MW00603816

Rivers and ROADS

Transportation in Early America

PHOTOGRAPHY BY David M. Doody

TEXT BY Mary Miley Theobald

Colonial Williamsburg

The Colonial Williamsburg Foundation
Williamsburg, Virginia

Reflect on the images in this book, not only with your eyes. Hear the soft cadence of unshod hooves on packed earth, the splash of a paddle into placid water, the scrape of an iron-rimmed wheel on a sandy road. Inhale the scent of a woodland spring or a new leather saddle on a spirited steed. Taste the crisp winter air after a snowfall or a mug of ale at a ferryman's tavern. Feel the jolt of a carriage on rutted roads and the gentle canter of a placid mare. Travel back in time to colonial Virginia.

The paths and waterways of the Chesapeake were formed long before the English adventurers arrived in 1607. Natives of Tsenacommacah, as the Indians called this region, had, for untold centuries, been traveling on foot and by paddle from village to village for purposes of trade, social interactions, and war until their slender wilderness paths had widened into trails a foot and a half across, and the tidewater streams and rivers had become as familiar as a pond.

From the Native Americans came the best form of watercraft. Hollowed-log canoes, called *pirogues* by the colonists, could slip into the shallowest of streams, though they could also continue onto the broad, tidal rivers flowing into the Chesapeake Bay. As the English groped their way inland, planting settlements that hugged the riverbanks, most travel was by boat. Pirogues and small sailing vessels—sloops, schooners, pinnaces, barks, ketches—were as vital as today's family car, connecting remote settlements to the colonial capital at Jamestown.

Rivers also provided routes west into Indian territory where Englishmen could pursue the riches of the fur trade, the most profitable enterprise, after tobacco, in Virginia. Forts built at the fall lines of the great rivers served as centers where Englishmen swapped cloth, copper, beads, and hatchets with natives for furs and deerskins. Later, traders like William Byrd I traveled far into the interior on horseback, following Indian trails through the mountains with caravans of heavily laden packhorses.

The abundance of rivers and streams in eastern Virginia dictated the colony's development. As a London publication of 1649 noted, "Most of their Plantations" were situated "upon the Rivers sides or up little Creeks, and but a small way into the Land." Seventy-five years later, little had changed. "No Country is better watered," explained the Reverend Hugh Jones in *The Present State of Virginia,* "for the Conveniency of which most Houses are built near some Landing-Place; so that any Thing may be delivered to a Gentleman there from

London, Bristol, &c." With such hospitable waterways, who needed roads? The plentiful streams and rivers actually hindered development of a road network because so many expensive ferries and bridges would be required to cross them all.

For colonists who needed to travel, choices were simple: walk, go by boat, ride a horse, or ride in a carriage. The commonest means of travel throughout the entire colonial era was by foot. Small sailboats and canoes were low-cost alternatives that could cover greater distances,

transport personal effects, and cross to the opposite side of a river. Horses were not an option for travelers during the colony's earliest years. The few horses brought on ships from England to Jamestown in 1609 were eaten during the Starving Time. Not a single carriage existed in the colony during its first few decades. The simple two-wheeled carts and four-wheeled wagons needed for agriculture were constructed on-site by planters or their indentured servants, although their iron-rimmed wheels were usually imported from England. "The earliest

wheeled vehicles," according to Paul Zelesnikar, Colonial Williamsburg journeyman wheelwright, "were the gun carriages, farm carts, and wheelbarrows at Jamestown."

Later shipments of horses survived and multiplied. By the middle of the seventeenth century, about 200 horses provided a means of transportation as well as the labor to pull plows and wagons. Oxen, the working cattle, were also used as draft animals. They, more than horses, were the main movers of heavy loads. Usually steers, oxen were probably as numerous as horses in early Virginia, and certainly as useful. But by the beginning of the eighteenth century, horses had become common, so much so that one Swiss visitor noted, "It must be a poor man who cannot afford one. Not many people can be seen traveling on foot, even if it is only an hour's distance. They are seldom used to draw wagons or the plow." Oxen were still preferred for that role. At the end of the colonial period, about 200,000 horses served a population of 748,000 in Virginia. George Washington owned 130 horses in 1785, which he used for farm

work, pulling carriages, riding, racing, foxhunting, and breeding. His favorite colors were white and dapple gray.

European visitors to Virginia often praised the quality of the colony's horses. One Englishman who visited Virginia in the 1770s raved, "Indeed nothing can be more elegant and beautiful than the horses bred here, either for the turf, the field, the road, or the coach; and they have always fine long, full, flowing tails." But another professed horror at the way Virginians mismatched their steeds: "They have no Concern about the different Colours of their Coach Horses, driving frequently black, white, and chesnut, in the same Harness."

Virginia's population had grown enough by the 1630s to require links among outlying communities—links that did not depend on wind and water. More Englishmen were settling on less convenient tracts of land far from navigable waterways. Hogsheads of tobacco and furs had to be delivered to ships bound for England. Planters had to journey to Jamestown on government business. People wanted to visit

neighboring plantations. The gentry needed to receive supplies and manufactured goods from England to trumpet their success: fashionable furniture, tea services, exotic fabrics, and, yes, carriages. While paths were suitable for foot travel by man or horse, roads were necessary for wheeled vehicles.

Englishmen began broadening existing Powhatan Indian paths into narrow roadways. In 1632, the Virginia General Assembly enacted America's first road law, ordering each county to lay out roads in "convenient places." Legislation also required each man to work on the roads a certain number of days each year or to pay another to work in his place—a feudal custom familiar to all. Some form of this law would remain in effect for the next 250 years, providing the main source of labor for road maintenance and bridge building.

While the abundant rivers were a blessing for boats, they were a curse for roads. Shallow creeks and streams could be forded—troublesome when the water was low and dangerous when the water ran deep and swift—

but crossing broad rivers like the James required ferries, which were sometimes nothing more than crude rafts. Soon after passing the first road legislation, the General Assembly tried to establish a system of free river ferries to be paid for out of tax revenues. Small landowners protested the expense. A revised plan set fares for pedestrians and horses, allowed the ferryman a tavern license, and exempted him from other public service, such as attending militia musters and maintaining roads.

By the beginning of the eighteenth century, fourteen ferries crossed the James River, an equal number crossed the York, and there were six on the Rappahannock. Convenience was elusive. Travelers might have to shoot guns or light fires to alert the ferryman on the opposite shore to come pick them up, and foul weather or floods could cause delays of a day or more. As time went on and money came available, bridges replaced ferries. Today Virginia still operates four ferries, all of them free.

Shortly before the Revolutionary War, a new craft appeared on the upper James River. Called *bateaux* after

the French word for "boats," these long, flat-bottomed vessels each carried as many as ten hogsheads of tobacco downriver to the busy port at Richmond. Rudderless, they were propelled by men using poles. Later, canals, along which barges could be pulled by mules, and trains made bateaux obsolete.

Not all roads followed Indian trails. The Virginia General Assembly appointed "Surveyors of highways" in 1662 to "lay out the most convenient wayes to the church, to the court, to James Towne, and from county to county, and make the said wayes forty foote broad, and make bridges where there is occasion." Forty-foot widths proved a bit too ambitious, so after the capital moved to Williamsburg in 1699, the Assembly reduced the requirement to thirty. "The most frequent users of roads were the locals with their carts and wagons," said Richard Nicoll, Colonial Williamsburg's director of Coach and Livestock. "For longer distances, freight wagons replaced in part the use of packhorses." Regular maintenance of these dirt roads included cutting away

A bateau on the James River

fallen trees, removing stumps, and repairing bridges.

The best-known colonial road was probably Three Notch'd, or Three Chopt, Road, the main east-west artery that ran from the fall line of the James River near Richmond to the Blue Ridge Mountains. Originally called Mountain Road, it took its later name from the system of marks it received during the 1740s. Based in part on Indian trails and surveyed in part by Thomas Jefferson's father, Three Notch'd Road served Virginians for two centuries before it was straightened during the Great Depression into Route 250. Today, Interstate 64 follows essentially the same route.

With wider, better-maintained roads came carriages, the general term for a wheeled, horse-drawn vehicle that carries passengers. The ones that first appeared in Virginia in the late 1600s were purely for show. The extravagance of a carriage conveyed its owner's status the way a private jet would today. Colonial governors were the most likely individuals to own carriages: Governor Sir William Berkeley of Green Spring, who died in 1677,

owned a coach, a type of four-wheeled carriage that could accommodate four to six people, during his later years. William Fitzhugh, the wealthy Stafford County planter who died in 1701, owned two. In 1710, Governor Alexander Spotswood showed off his own coach on short drives around Williamsburg, from the Palace to the coffeehouse, taverns, or the Capitol.

By the 1720s, carriages no longer turned heads on the streets of cities like Boston, Philadelphia, New York, Charleston, Baltimore, or even Williamsburg, where most prosperous merchants and planters indulged in a carriage or two. But poor roads made their use outside these cities risky. Road quality in Tidewater Virginia may have been better than that of other colonies, perhaps due to the level terrain and the sandy soil that allowed for good drainage. The Reverend Hugh Jones noted in 1724 that the roads were "in a pleasant, dry, sandy Soil, free from Stones and Dirt, and shaded and sheltered chiefly by Trees." About a dozen years later, another traveler wrote, "The Avenues leading to *Williamsburgh, Norfolk,* &c.

are prodigiously agreeable. . . . some of the best I ever saw, and infinitely superior to most in *England."* And yet others pronounced them "so bad . . . it's scarce possible to drive." Which was it? "I like to tell guests that roads back then were like roads today," said Zelesnikar. "Some were good; some were awful." Bad weather could render even the best road impassable.

Road conditions and the weather probably explain why Virginia horses generally went unshod, at least during the first century of settlement. Because of the good roads, wrote one visitor in 1688, "they ride their Horses without shooing them . . . the Country and Clime being dry, their Hoofs are much harder." Another noted that horseshoes were "seldom used in the lower Parts of the Country, where there are few Stones" but had to be used when horses were taken west into the mountains. At least some horses were partially shod: "shoes on his fore feet," say numerous advertisements for lost horses. "His hind Feet were lately shod," says another.

By the eighteenth century, serviceable roads made

stage wagons a feasible mode of transportation. Forerunner to the stagecoach, the stage wagon was a wagon fitted with benches and an overhead covering and pulled by four to eight horses. They traveled in stages, pausing at regular intervals for fresh horses. They provided transportation between the larger colonial cities for those who didn't have their own conveyance. The rides could be treacherous and were certain to be uncomfortable. Passengers had to descend at every ferry crossing and horse change and might have to walk—or push—when going uphill. George Washington noted in 1775 that, while there was no stage travel south of Virginia, a person could, if fortunate, travel by stage from Richmond to Boston in ten or twelve days.

The distance a person could travel in a day depended on many factors, including the weather, the condition of the roads, and the number of rivers to be crossed. It took George Washington anywhere from three to seven days to ride his horse from Mount Vernon to Williamsburg, something a car can accomplish in under

three hours. Carriage travel was even slower than horseback. Well into the nineteenth century, a boat was the best choice for longer distances.

Two-wheeled carts and four-wheeled wagons were used for transporting heavy loads, with the drivers usually walking alongside the horses or oxen that pulled them. Passenger vehicles were never numerous, but in Virginia the most familiar was the lightweight, two-wheeled riding chair for one or two people, probably because it was the least expensive and needed only a

single horse to pull it. Chairs outnumbered coaches by three or four to one. Riding in a carriage was certain to be an unsettling experience, as its wooden seats lacked padding, and springs didn't come into use until the middle of the eighteenth century. Most used leather straps to minimize jolting. "If persons wish to travel with comfort," wrote Issac Weld, who visited Virginia in the 1790s, "they ought always to set out provided with cushions for their hips and elbows, otherwise they cannot expect but to receive numberless contusions."

When President Washington toured the southern states in 1791, he rode in a chariot, a carriage with a single seat for up to three people, pulled by four horses, trailed by a baggage wagon pulled by two horses, and accompanied by four saddle mounts and one extra horse that someone led. An enslaved coachman drove the chariot, and another slave rode "postilion," that is, on one of the horses of the chariot team.

Carts and wagons could be hammered together on the farm or plantation by self-taught men, but the construction and repair of carriages involved a prodigious number of tradesmen, including harnessmakers, blacksmiths, cabinetmakers, painters, carvers, gilders, varnishers, brass founders, spring makers, and upholsterers. While some Virginians, such as George Wythe and George Washington, preferred to order their conveyances from England to assure they were getting the latest fashion, many hired local wheelwrights or coachmakers, thus saving the expense of bringing the vehicle across the Atlantic.

One such local man was Elkanah Deane, who lived and worked near the Governor's Palace. Apprenticed in Dublin, a center of coachmaking with a reputation rivaling that of London, Deane moved to New York in 1764 where the governor, the Earl of Dunmore, became a customer. In 1771, King George III appointed Lord Dunmore governor of Virginia. Skilled and ambitious, Deane followed his patron south the following year and set up shop in Williamsburg.

Robert Carter of Nomini Hall in Virginia's Northern Neck, one of the colony's wealthiest planters, ordered most of his manufactured goods from England, including his carriage. His children's tutor, Philip Vickers Fithian, wrote excitedly in his journal in 1774 when the fine, new vehicle was delivered: "Arrived this afternoon our new Coach—It is a plain carriage, upper part black, lower Sage or Pea-Green—The Harness is neat strong, & suitable for the Country. Price 120£ Sterling." That amount would also have purchased eight hundred gallons of rum or paid a journeyman's wages for four years.

When Fithian first arrived in Virginia from New Jersey, he had noticed a strange custom among the women who traveled in carriages: "Almost every Lady wears a red Cloak; and when they ride out they tye a white handkerchief over their Head and face, so that when I first came into Virginia, I was distress'd whenever I saw a Lady, for I thought She had the Tooth-Ach!"

All of the governors who lived in the Palace owned a coach and several other sorts of carriage, usually including a chariot. So did prominent Williamsburg residents like Robert Carter Nicholas, John Randolph, Benjamin Waller, George Wythe, and Edward Ambler. For those who could not afford their own vehicles, rentals were available. Tavern keepers often rented horses and carriages to patrons. In 1745, Joseph Gilliam, a Williamsburg entrepreneur, advertised a "very good travelling Chair and Horses, to hire to any Part of the Country: Also a Cart and Horses."

America's coachmaking industry began in the eighteenth century and flourished until it was eclipsed by

the automobile industry. Coachmaking started up again in Williamsburg in the 1970s with a small wheelwright's shop tasked initially with repairing the colonial-style vehicles. Over the years, the shop expanded until it is, today, fully engaged in the manufacture of two-wheeled carriages, carts, and wagons. Wheelwrights split their time between their shop on the Elkanah Deane property and the Public Armoury, where they build specialized vehicles for military use. "During the Revolution, the army would often confiscate vehicles for their own use,"

explained John Boag, master wheelwright, "but they also ordered specialized vehicles made, like gun carriages, heavier carts and wagons, and wheelbarrows." Civilian vehicles are built from scratch and even upholstered and painted at the shop. In the tradition of John Durand, a colonial portrait painter who advertised that "he will also paint, gild, and varnish, wheel carriages; and put coats of arms, or ciphers, upon them," journeyman Andrew DeLisle mixes paints according to eighteenth-century recipes and does a good deal of the painting.

Despite cavalry and coaches, for most soldiers in the Continental army travel meant marching. Sometimes they marched to the music of fifes and drums, but marching was only occasionally a celebratory parade. One soldier, Joseph Plumb Martin, complained of being "forced to march many a weary mile in winter, through cold and snow." To reach Yorktown for the crucial siege of British forces, Washington's troops traveled almost four hundred miles.

Today's visitors find a wide array of vehicles on Williamsburg's busy streets, including two sociables, two town coaches, a traveling coach, a stage wagon, a chariot, a landau, and two riding chairs. Between twenty-five and thirty horses are maintained to pull them and other horse carts and wagons. Two pairs of sturdy oxen haul the oxcarts and wagons.

Travel in colonial America—whether by boat, horse, carriage, or foot—often involved hardship, occasionally brought pleasure, but always meant adventure.

"The rivers are so propitious to the nature and use of man."

-John Smith, 1612

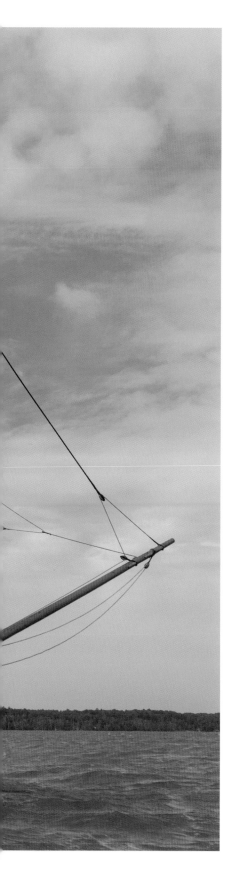

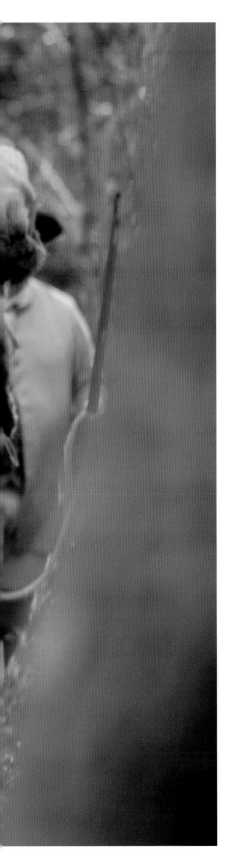

" The morning was fine, & Nomini-River alive with Boats Canoes &c some going to Church, some fishing, & some Sporting. "

-Philip Vickers Fithian, 1774

"The larger the wheels of the *waggon*, . . . the easier the motion. . . . But still, the higher a *waggon*, &c. is set, the apter it is to overturn."

—Chambers's *Cyclopaedia*, 1743

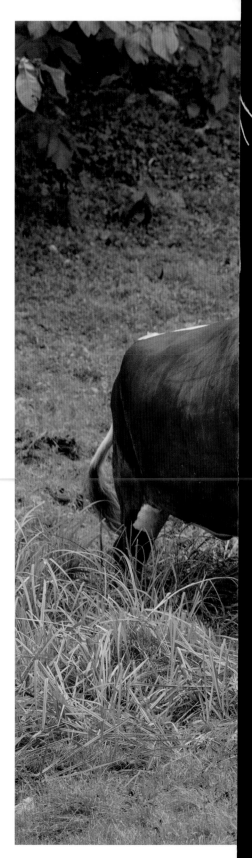

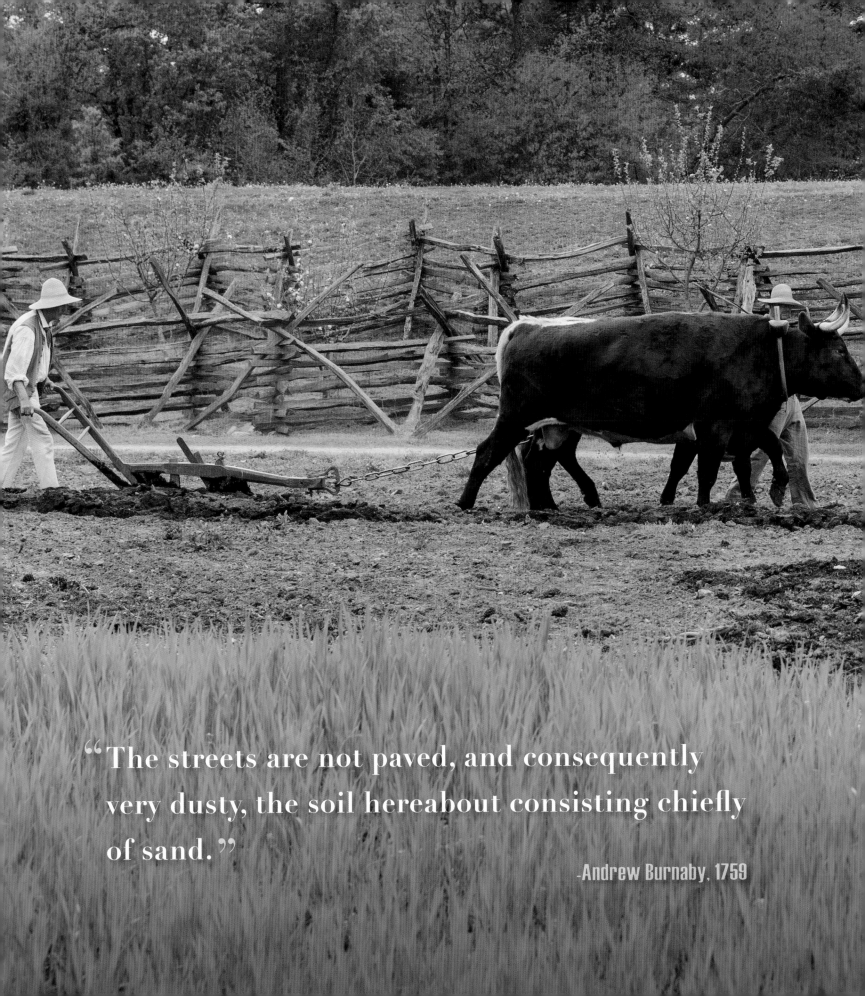

"The streets are not paved, and consequently very dusty, the soil hereabout consisting chiefly of sand."

-Andrew Burnaby, 1759

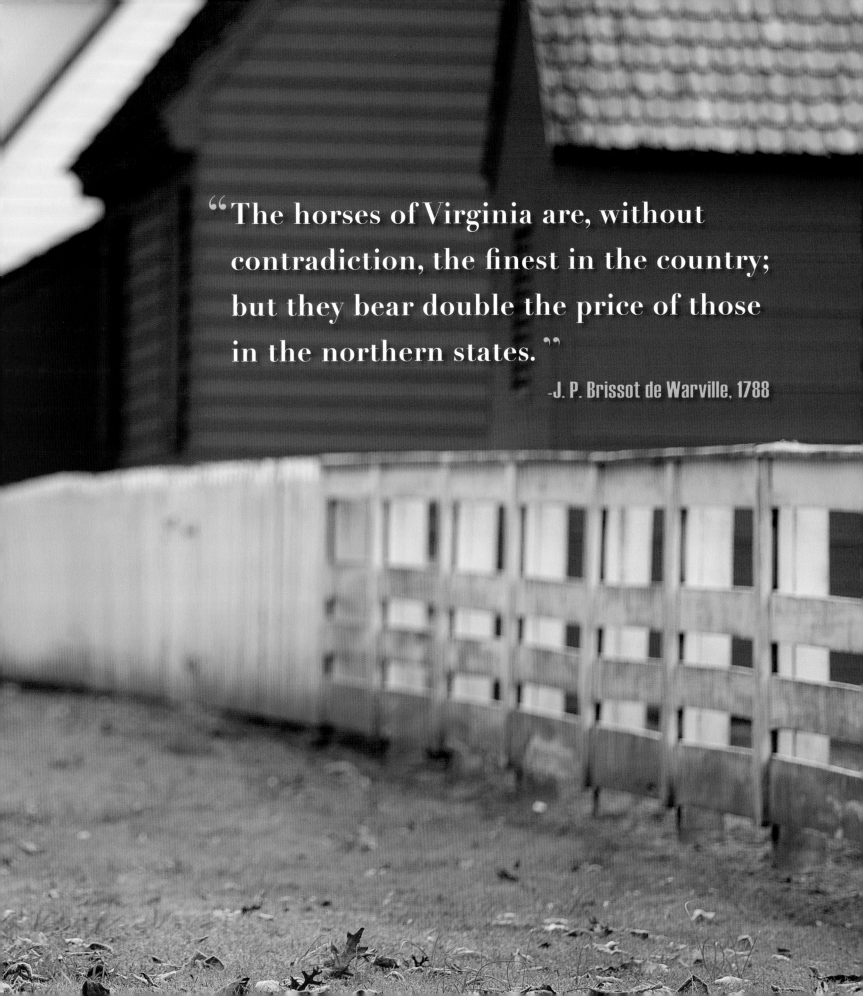

"The horses of Virginia are, without contradiction, the finest in the country; but they bear double the price of those in the northern states."

-J. P. Brissot de Warville, 1788

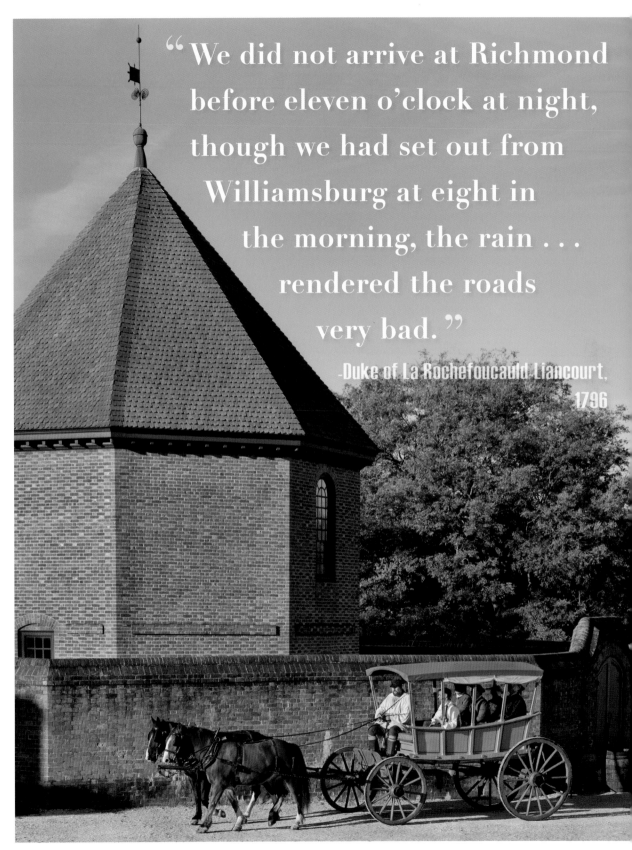

"We did not arrive at Richmond before eleven o'clock at night, though we had set out from Williamsburg at eight in the morning, the rain . . . rendered the roads very bad."

–Duke of La Rochefoucauld-Liancourt, 1796

"Riding in a carriage was like riding in a boat."

-Paul Zelesnikar, 2014

FURTH FORTUNE

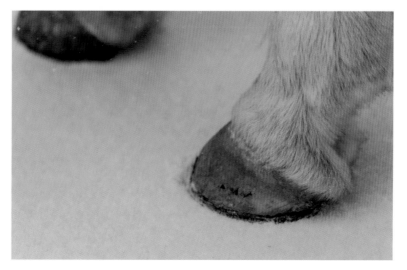

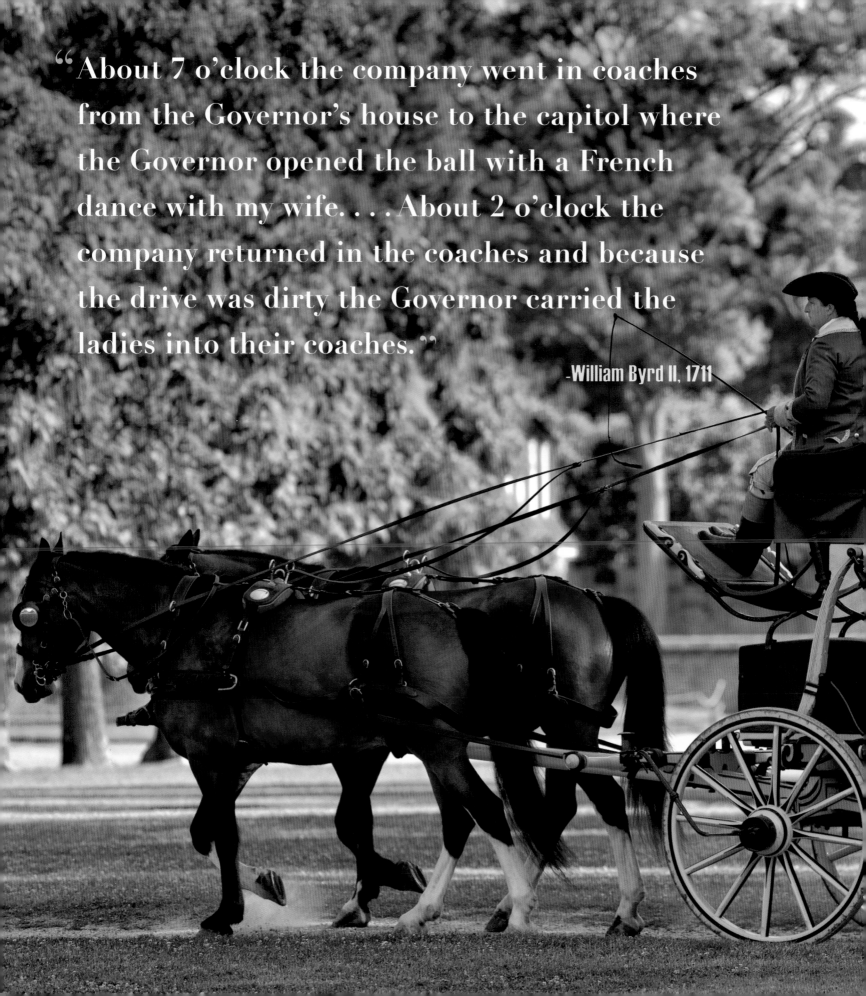

"About 7 o'clock the company went in coaches from the Governor's house to the capitol where the Governor opened the ball with a French dance with my wife. . . . About 2 o'clock the company returned in the coaches and because the drive was dirty the Governor carried the ladies into their coaches."

—William Byrd II, 1711

" . . . the prodigious Number of Coaches that croud the deep, sandy Streets of this little City."

-Edward Kimber, 1746

"Of all the exercises walking is best.
A horse gives but a kind of half exercise,
and a carriage is no better than a cradle."

-Thomas Jefferson, 1786

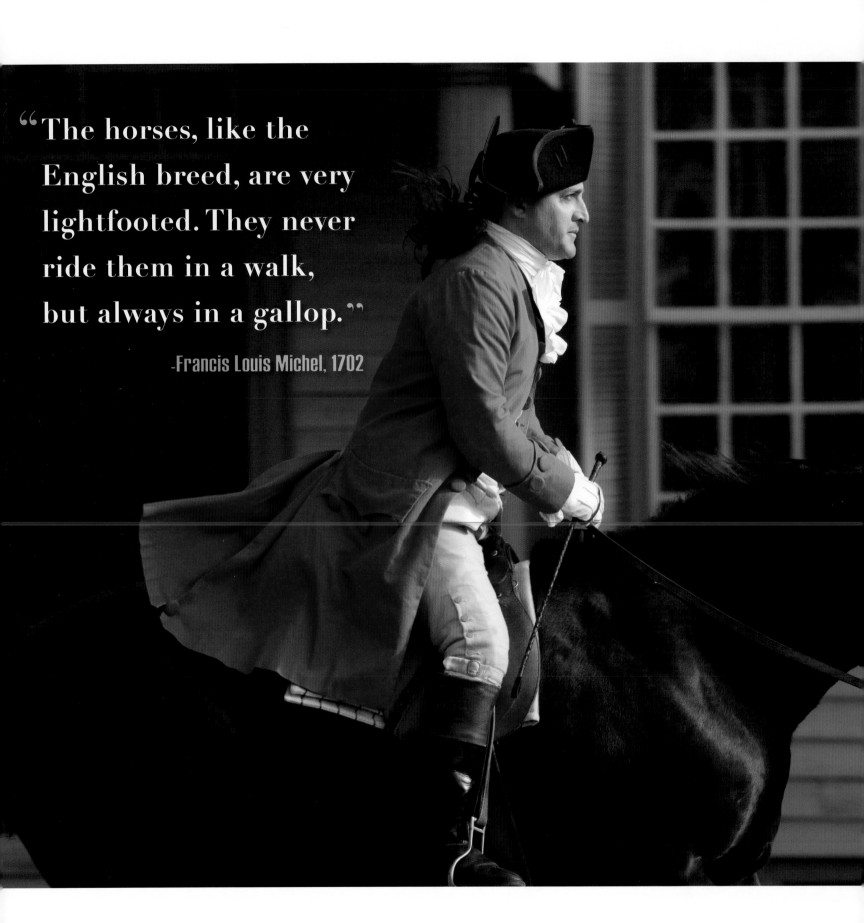

"The horses, like the English breed, are very lightfooted. They never ride them in a walk, but always in a gallop."

-Francis Louis Michel, 1702

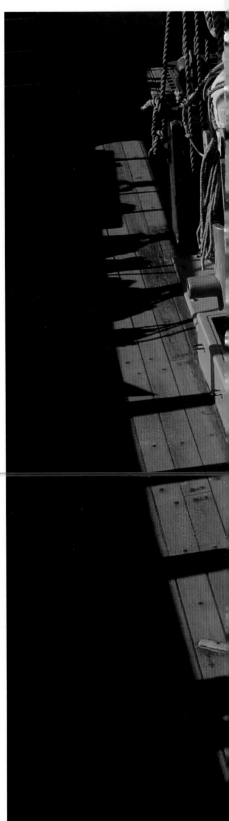

To see my Friends some Distance out of Town,

In the Stage-Coach I took a Passage down;

. . . .

From [a] blest Vision was I snatcht away,

To suffer more than I find Words to say.

The Travellers were met, and 'twixt a Brace

Of fat old Dames I squeez'd into my Place;

A Matron, with a Child, on t'other Side,

A Serjeant too, with more than decent Pride,

Was seated; to compleat the rueful Scene,

A Vintner cramm'd his bloated Carcass in:

Condemn'd in such Society to go,

What Pen, what Pencil, can describe my Woe?

. . . .

A Fit of Coughing one old Lady shook,

At which a Fit of Scolding t'other took.

The Soldier swore, to prove his dauntless Heart,

Young Master puk'd, and gave us all a Part.

. . . .

If one was sure in each Stage-Coach to meet

A Company so sociable, so sweet,

E'er I would trouble them again with mine,

Instead of riding One Mile, I'd walk nine.

Excerpted from "The Stage-Coach from Bourn, Imitated,"

in the *Maryland Gazette*, October 13, 1757

Acknowledgments

Many people contributed to this book. Key to most of the photography was Richard Nicoll, director of Coach and Livestock at Colonial Williamsburg until he retired in 2015. His constant support, enthusiasm, and shared vision for the project gave us access to livestock, vehicles, and his and his staff's expertise. Thanks to Bill White, Colonial Williamsburg's vice president of Productions, Publications, and Learning Ventures, and Bill Wagner, executive producer and director of Media Services, for giving me the time and freedom to pursue this project. Colonial Williamsburg's Barbara Tyler-Mullins and Jae White scheduled in-house models and locations, and Rebecca Scheetz kept us organized, researched outside locations and models, obtained permits, and handled many other details. A special thanks to the crew of the *Rose of Nelson* bateau; it took us three tries over a year before river conditions allowed us on the water to photograph them, but persistence paid off. Buck Woodard and Willie Balderson of Colonial Williamsburg's Department of Public History worked tirelessly with us on the complex shoots involving Indians with canoes in two different time periods, in multiple locations, and trading with the English. Their expert knowledge was vital to creating historically accurate photos. The staff of Colonial Williamsburg's Photo Services department was a constant support throughout the project, particularly Tom Green and Darnell Vennie, who assisted on many of the shoots.

Most importantly I want to express my thanks to Cherry and Eddie Robinson. Without their generous gifts funding the photography and the publication of the book, none of this would have been possible.

-Dave Doody

The publication of this volume was made possible by a generous gift from Cherry and Eddie Robinson of Williamsburg, Virginia.

© 2015 by The Colonial Williamsburg Foundation
All rights reserved. Published 2015.

25 24 23 22 21 20 19 18 17 16 15   1 2 3 4 5 6

Library of Congress Cataloging-in-Publication Data

Theobald, Mary Miley, 1952- author.
  Rivers and roads : transportation in early America / photography by David M. Doody ; text by Mary Miley Theobald.
    pages cm
  ISBN 978-0-87935-277-6 (hardcover : alk. paper) 1. Transportation--Virginia--History. 2. Inland water transportation--Virginia--History. 3.
Inland waterway vessels--Virginia--History. 4. Trails--Virginia--History. 5. Roads--Virginia--History. I. Doody, David M., photographer. II. Title.

  HE213.V8T44 2015
  388.09755'09032--dc23

             2015004857

Printed in the United States of America

Designed by Shanin Glenn

The Colonial Williamsburg Foundation is the not-for-profit center for history and citizenship.

Colonial Williamsburg® is a registered trade name of The Colonial Williamsburg Foundation.

The Colonial Williamsburg Foundation
PO Box 1776
Williamsburg, Virginia 23187-1776
colonialwilliamsburg.org

The Jamestown-Yorktown Foundation granted permission for photos to be taken of the *Discovery* and the *Godspeed,* re-creations of two of the three ships that brought America's first permanent English colonists to Virginia in 1607. The ships are on exhibit at Jamestown Settlement history museum. The photos appear on pages 24–27 and 80–81. James City County and its Parks and Recreation Department granted permission for photos to be taken at its Powhatan Creek and Chickahominy Riverfront parks. These appear on pages 4–5, 22–23, 30–31, and 86–91. The National Park Service granted permission for photos to be taken at Historic Jamestowne and on the Colonial Parkway. These appear on the jacket and pages 28–29, 50, and 92–93. The York River State Park granted permission for the photos on pages 32–33. George Washington's Mount Vernon granted permission to take the photo appearing on page 16. The photos of the bateau on pages 10–11 and 36–37 are of the *Rose of Nelson.*